The White-Tailed Deer

by Michael Zwaschka

Reading Consultant:
Mike Hansen
North American Hunting Club

CAPSTONE PRESS
MANKATO, MINNESOTA

C A P S T O N E　　P R E S S
818 North Willow Street • Mankato, Minnesota 56001

Printed in the United States of America.

Library of Congress Cataloging-in-Publication Data
Zwaschka, Michael.
    The white-tailed deer/by Michael Zwaschka.
    p. cm.-- (Wildlife of North America)
    Includes bibliographical references (p. 45) and index.
    Summary: Details the characteristics, habitat, and life cycle of the white-tailed deer.
    ISBN 1-56065-365-5
    1. White-tailed deer--Juvenile literature. [1. White-tailed deer. 2. Deer.]
I. Title. II. Series.
QL737.U55Z94
599.65'2'097--dc21

96-48685
CIP
AC

Photo credits
Visuals Unlimited/Gary Carter, cover, 16, 19, 41;
    Joe McDonald, 24; Leonard Lee Rue, 47
Root Resources/Alan G. Nelson, 8, 26; Jim Nachel, 22;
    Kenneth Fink, 34
Daybreak Imagery/Richard Day, 6, 10,
William Muñoz, 30, 32, 45
William B. Folsom, 14, 20
Lynn M. Stone, 12, 28
Charles Melton, 38-39
FPG, 9

Table of Contents

Fast Facts about White-Tailed Deer.................... 4

Chapter 1 The White-Tailed Deer...................... 7

Chapter 2 Survival Habits................................ 13

Chapter 3 Life Cycle... 25

Chapter 4 White-Tailed Deer and People 33

Photo Diagram... 38

Words to Know 42

To Learn More 43

Useful Addresses 44

Internet Sites 46

Index 48

Pronunciation guides follow difficult words, both in the text and in the
Words to Know section in the back of the book.

Fast Facts about White-Tailed Deer

Scientific Name: Odocoileus Virginianus

Height: In the northern United States and Canada, adult male deer grow to at least 41 inches (103 centimeters) tall from the ground to the shoulders.

Weight: Adult male deer in the northern United States and Canada weigh about 160 pounds (72 kilograms).

Physical Features: White-tailed deer have white hair on the underside of their tails.

Habits: White-tailed deer are shy and cautious. They feed at dawn and dusk. They communicate with other white-tailed deer through sounds and actions.

Food: White-tailed deer will eat almost any kind of plant to survive. They eat tree buds, leaves, and grasses in spring. They eat acorns, chestnuts, and blackberries in summer. They eat tree bark and twigs during winter.

Reproduction: The mating season for white-tailed deer is late fall. A new deer is called a fawn. Fawns are born in spring. A female deer is called a doe. A doe has one fawn the first time she mates. The second time she may have twins.

Range: White-tailed deer live in the United States, southern Canada, Mexico, and Central America.

Habitat: White-tailed deer live in deserts, swamps, forests, farmlands, and prairies. They prefer to live in open areas next to rivers, streams, or lakes.

State Symbols: The white-tailed deer is the state animal for Illinois, New Hampshire, Ohio, Pennsylvania, and South Carolina. It is the state wildlife animal for Wisconsin. The white-tailed deer is Nebraska's state mammal and Mississippi's state land mammal.

Chapter 1

The White-Tailed Deer

Thirty-eight types of white-tailed deer live in the United States, southern Canada, Mexico, and Central America. The white-tailed deer is one of the largest populations of hoofed animals in North America. In 1900, the white-tailed deer population in the United States was 500,000. Today, the population has increased to 18 million.

White-tailed deer can adapt to people and learn to live almost anywhere. They live in and near cities. They live on farm land. They also live in wooded areas near streams, rivers, and

Today the white-tailed deer population is 18 million.

White-tailed deer living in colder climates are larger than those living in warmer climates.

lakes. They prefer the edges of wooded areas. This is where most berries grow and the grass is thickest. Trees also provide good hiding places for white-tailed deer.

Usually, white-tailed deer live alone. During the winter, they travel in herds. A herd is a group of animals. A herd provides safety from predators that can easily catch white-tailed deer in winter. A predator is any animal that eats other animals to survive.

A male deer is called a buck. A female deer is called a doe. A newborn deer is called a fawn. A one-year-old deer is called a yearling.

Size

The white-tailed deer belongs to the deer family, which includes caribou, elk, moose, and mule deer. The white-tailed deer is the smallest member of the deer family. A white-tailed deer's size depends on where it lives.

White-tailed deer living in cold climates are larger than those living in warm climates. A larger animal holds more body heat. White-tailed deer living in the northern United States have bigger bodies than those living

DEER TRACKS

Walking   Running

The white-tailed deer's most defining characteristic is the white hair on the underside of its tail.

in the southern United States. Animals lose body heat through their legs, ears, and tails. White-tailed deer in cold climates have shorter legs, ears, and tails than those living in warm climates.

In northern United States and Canada, full-grown bucks stand about 41 inches (104 centimeters) tall, measured from the ground to the shoulder. Bucks weigh an average of 160 pounds (72 kilograms). Large bucks can weigh up to 300 pounds (135 kilograms). Key deer live in Florida. They are a type of white-tailed deer. They measure about 28 inches (71 centimeters) tall. Full-grown key bucks weigh about 80 pounds (36 kilograms).

Characteristics

White-tailed deer may live in and near populated areas. But they are still shy and cautious animals. They are always aware of their surroundings. Any sounds or movements alert them to danger. Running and sharp senses are their main defense.

White-tailed deer signal other white-tailed deer with sounds and actions when they sense danger. They try to avoid predators by being quiet when they search for food.

The white-tailed deer's most defining characteristic is the white hair on the underside of their tails. When white-tailed deer are afraid, they raise their tails. The white underside of the tail signals danger to other deer.

White-tailed deer use their speed to protect themselves from predators. They can run at speeds of 40 miles (64 kilometers) per hour.

Chapter 2

Survival Habits

White-tailed deer can live almost anywhere. They live in deserts, swamps, forests, farmlands, and prairies. Generally, deer need a lot of space to roam. Growing cities and populations have driven elk and mule deer to remote areas. But white-tailed deer can live in more populated areas.

Some white-tailed deer become so used to people that they live near people's homes. Others live on farmland and in wooded areas. White-tailed deer feed in farmers' fields.

The high population of white-tailed deer has caused problems. They can eat entire flower and vegetable gardens. Hungry deer can destroy wooded areas by eating young trees. This is a sign

White-tailed deer can live in deserts, swamps, forests, and farmlands.

that deer cannot find enough food. If there is not enough food many deer starve.

Feeding Habits

White-tailed deer's feeding habits can vary depending on the situation. During the summer, they eat greens such as bushes and grasses. Eating grasses is called grazing. White-tailed deer prefer to graze at the edge of wooded areas and open fields.

In late fall and winter, white-tailed deer will eat plants with woody stems, including tree buds, leaves and twigs. White-tailed deer sometimes stand on their hind legs to reach for leaves and buds in trees.

Predators like to attack when white-tailed deer are feeding. The deer are busy gathering tree leaves, buds, and grasses. It is difficult for them to hear and smell predators.

White-tailed deer sometimes graze in open fields. Wolves and coyotes can easily see white-tailed deer in an open field. So white-tailed deer feed in the early morning or late

White-tailed deer eat greens in the summer. In the winter, they eat plants with woody stems.

evening. The dim light at these times of day helps them hide from predators.

During heavy hunting times, white-tailed deer stay hidden during the day. They feed only at night.

White-tailed deer also avoid predators by quickly gathering food and moving to another spot. The movement makes it harder for predators to track white-tailed deer. This gives white-tailed deer a chance to notice predators.

White-tailed deer do not fully chew their food right away. They bite leaves and buds off tree limbs. They eat grasses and bushes. Then, they swallow the food into one of their four stomachs and save it for later.

After white-tailed deer gather food in their stomachs, they find a safe place to fully chew their food. They spit up the half-digested food and chew it. Half-digested food is called cud. Then, the deer swallow their cud into another stomach to finish digesting it.

After a white-tailed deer gathers food in its stomach, it finds a safe place to fully chew it.

White-tailed deer feed heavily before bad weather. They have a way of knowing when a cold front is on the way. They know 12 to 24 hours before a storm arrives.

Sharp Senses

White-tailed deer rely on a keen sense of smell. Every white-tailed deer has its own scent. Scent glands are located near the deer's eyes and hooves, and behind the legs. A mother deer tells her fawns apart by their scent. White-tailed deer continually sniff the air to detect the scent of a predator.

White-tailed deer see in black and white. In black and white, an animal or person standing still blends into the background. But, white-tailed deer can detect the slightest movement. When they detect movement, they stand still, look, and listen.

White-tailed deer use speed to escape approaching predators, such as coyotes, lynx, and wolves. They can run up to 40 miles (64 kilometers) per hour. They can also jump over

When a white-tailed deer detects movement, it stands still, looks, and listens.

fences or logs about eight and one-half feet
(two and one-half meters) high.

When white-tailed deer sense danger, they
stomp their feet and grunt to warn others.
When other white-tailed deer hear these grunts,
their white tails go up. They run into the woods
or across an open field. Predators know that
white-tailed deer will not be easy to catch if
they are running. The deer are too fast.

Winter Survival

Winter is a difficult time for deer, especially in
colder climates. Food is limited. White-tailed
deer must search harder to find food.

During the summer, white-tailed deer
prepare for fall and winter. They eat a lot of
food. Green shoots, leaves, and buds are easy
to find during summer. The deer build up a
layer of fat to help keep them warm in winter.

In late summer, deer also shed their fur.
They begin to grow a second coat. The new
coat grows in thicker and warmer for winter.

White-tailed deer must look harder to find food in winter.

The new coat turns a different color. In the spring and summer, the white-tailed deer's coats are reddish-brown. In the winter, their coats look more grayish-brown.

Each hair on a deer's coat is hollow. The hollow hair is filled with air. This helps deer stay warm in cold weather.

Most of the year, white-tailed deer travel alone. During winter, they gather in herds in low areas to move out of the wind. They leave the low, sheltered areas only to find food.

White-tailed deer's hooves sink in deep snow. This gives predators that run on top of snow a big advantage. Predators kill sick deer that cannot escape very well. Many older and weaker deer die in the winter. They are not strong enough to survive.

Each hair on a deer's coat is hollow. The hollow hair is filled with air. This helps a deer stay warm.

Chapter 3

Life Cycle

The mating season is called the rutting season. The first signs of the rut are found on trees. Scraped-off tree bark shows where bucks rubbed the velvet off their antlers. Antlers are bony horns that look like branches. Deer grow antlers on top of their heads. The antlers are covered with velvet.

Once their velvet sheds, the bucks attack trees and bushes. This helps them prepare to fight with other bucks.

Rutting Season
The rutting season takes place in fall. The biggest and strongest bucks in the herd mate.

A buck will rub the velvet off of its antlers in the fall.

They mate with anywhere from four to 20 does. The increased activity causes some bucks to lose about a quarter of their weight.

Bucks fight other bucks for the right to mate. Younger bucks rarely fight older, larger bucks. Younger bucks know who is stronger. When bucks want to mate, they scrape a spot on the ground with their hooves. Their hooves have a gland that creates a special scent. Bucks leave their scent on the scraped ground. A doe leaves her scent on the same scraped spot. Then the buck will come looking for her.

Two bucks will fight if they find the same doe. They push and stab each other with their antlers. Bucks can kill each other, or they could starve to death if their antlers lock together. Usually, though, one gives up.

Birth

White-tailed deer fawns are born in May or early June. A young doe can mate her first fall. A young doe may give birth to a single fawn when she is one year old. The ability to breed

White-tailed deer fawns are born in May or early June.

at such a young age quickly increases the white-tailed deer population.

A doe wants to be alone for birth. She finds a quiet place. She chases away other yearling or one-year-old fawns. Bucks are busy eating leaves and tree buds. They do not return after mating to help raise fawns. In the fall, bucks begin their new growth of antlers. They use these antlers to fight during mating season.

Protection from Predators

A newborn fawn has a scent right away. This makes it a target for predators. After birth, a doe licks her fawn clean to remove its scent. A fawn can stand within half an hour of its birth. It soon drinks its mother's milk. The milk is called colostrum (kul-AH-strum). Colostrum contains protein to help a fawn grow stronger.

A doe hides its fawn when it leaves to feed. White spots on the fawn's brown fur helps it hide in the brush.

Some does have twin fawns. A doe will separate its fawns when it leaves. That way, if a

White spots on a fawn's brown fur help it hide from predators

predator catches one, the other fawn may escape. A fawn bleats loudly if a predator attacks it. A doe may respond to its cries in one of two ways. First, the doe may fight off a predator. Second, it may try to get the predator to chase it instead of its fawn.

Growing Up

In summer, does raise their young. Fawns gain the most weight during summer. They learn to rely less on their mother's milk. They become more independent. Fawns play to become strong. They buck, kick, leap, and chase their mothers. Does also teach their fawns the important skill of hiding. Fawns begin to lose their spots in late summer. Their fur turns a brownish-gray color.

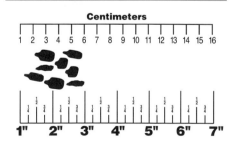

Scat, pictured below, is used to find out where an animal lives and what it eats.

Fawns gain the most weight during summer.

White-Tailed Deer and People

The swift and alert nature of white-tailed deer helps them escape predators. These characteristics can also be found in some people. Some North American Indians called the white-tailed deer's sharp senses deer medicine.

They believed that people who have deer medicine are sensitive and aware. They even thought some people had powers to see into the

White-tailed deer have a swift and alert nature.

future. People with deer medicine often move quickly. They never stay in one place for long. Some North American Indians believe that deer medicine brings beauty and grace to any surrounding.

Tribal Legends

North American Indians often told legends about animals. Legends are stories that are passed down through generations. Many North American Indian tribes used a turtle's shell as a calendar. A turtle's shell has about 13 scales. Thirteen full moons occur each year. They can be seen every 28 days.

The Winnebago Indians are Plains Indians. They call their 11th moon the Moon When Deer Drop Their Horns. This is the time of year when winter is about to begin.

The Winnebago legend says that deer banded together in their winter lodges during this time. The deer had just finished the rutting season, when they fought to prove who was the strongest.

A Winnebago legend explains why deer lose their antlers.

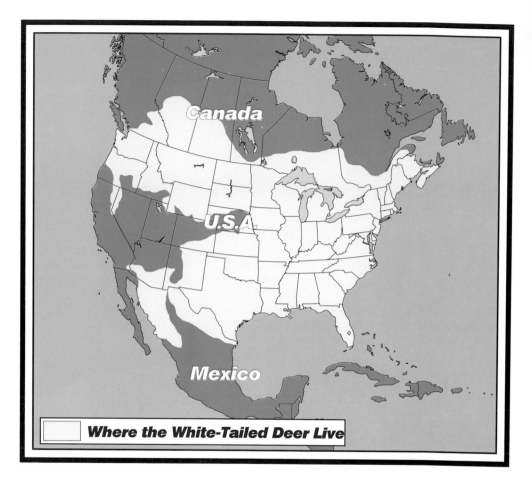

Where the White-Tailed Deer Live

    The Winnebagos say that at one time, deer kept their horns all year long. When the deer entered their winter lodge, they continued to fight. Because this caused deer to suffer, Earth

Maker sent his helper Na-na-bush to loosen the horns. Now each winter when the deer gather, they leave their weapons outside of the lodge.

Hunters as Helpers

In 1900, there were only 500,000 white-tailed deer. Today, about 18 million white-tailed deer roam the United States and Canada. The increase in population is due to the reduction of natural predators and some mild winters.

Wolves are natural predators of white-tailed deer. But people killed many wolves because they attacked livestock. The loss of wolves has seriously affected the white-tailed deer population. Wolves are not killing off as many sick deer. Then, disease spreads throughout the herds.

White-tailed deer do not have many natural predators. When white-tailed deer do not have many natural predators, the deer population grows quickly. This means less food. Deer starve if they cannot find food in long and cold northern winters.

Reddish-Brown Fur

White Tail

White Underside

Antlers

Sharp Hearing

Sharp Sense of Smell

Hooves

Deer hunters have tried to balance out the population of deer by hunting them each fall. This supplies the hunters with fresh meat. And the deer do not have to suffer from starvation in winter.

Many believe people can reduce the high white-tailed deer population by letting nature take its course. During long, cold northern winters, people sometimes put food outside for the deer. They may save a deer from starvation this winter, but they make more problems for the next winter. There will be even more deer and still less food.

Some people believe that the number of the white-tailed deer's natural predators should be allowed to increase. Then, if the animals are left alone, nature can become balanced again.

Deer hunters have tried to balance out the population of deer by hunting them each fall.

Words to Know

antler (ANT-lur)—a bony growth from a deer's head

buck—(BUHK)—a male deer

cud (KUHD)—half-digested food spit up and eaten again

doe (DOH)—a female deer

fawn (FAHWN)—a newborn deer

predator (PRED-uh-tur)—an animal that hunts other animals for food

prey (PRAY)—animals hunted for food

rut (RHUT)—to mate

scrape (SKRAPE)—a mark bucks make on the ground with their hooves.

velvet (VEL-vit)—a soft, furry skin that covers the antlers while they are growing.

yearling (YIRH-ling)—a one-year-old deer

To Learn More

Ahlstrom, Mark. *The White-Tailed Deer*. Mankato, Minn.: Crestwood House, 1983.

Arnowsky, Jim. *Secrets of a Wildlife Watcher*. New York: Lothrop, Lee & Shepard Books, 1983.

Baily, Jill. *Discovering Deer*. New York: The Bookwright Press, 1988.

Bruchac, Joseph and Jonathan London. *Thirteen Moons on Turtle's Back*. New York: Philomel Books, 1992.

Gamlin, Linda. *The Deer in the Forest*. Milwaukee: Gareth Stevens Publishing, 1988.

Hirschi, Ron. *Headgear*. New York: Dodd, Mead & Co., 1984.

Useful Addresses

Ministry of Natural Resources
435 James Street South
Thunder Bay, ON P7E 6E3
Canada

Minnesota Deer Hunters Association
P.O. Box 5123
Grand Rapids, MN 55744-5123

Minnesota Department of Natural Resources
500 Lafayette Road
St. Paul, MN 55155-4046

National Wildlife Federation
1412 Sixteenth Street NW
Washington, DC 20036

White-tailed deer stay alert while eating. They gather food quickly and keep moving so predators cannot follow them.

Internet Sites

Illinois State Animal
http://www.museum.state.il.us/exhibits/
symbols/animal.html

Kids—Learn about Deer
http://www.tpwd.state.tx.us/adv/kidspage/
animals/deer.htm

Powerful Animal Symbols
http://www.powersource.com/gallery/objects

Whitetails on the Web
http://www.io.com/~benton/wt.htm

White-tailed deer are shy and cautious.

Index

antler, 25

buck, 9-10, 25, 27, 29

Canada, 4-5, 7, 9
Central America, 5, 7
coat, 21, 23
colostrum, 29
cud, 17

doe, 9, 27, 29

elk, 9, 13

fawn, 5, 9, 27, 29, 31

height, 9-11
herd, 8-9, 23
hunter, 40

key deer, 11

legend, 35
livestock, 37

mating, 5, 25, 27, 29
Mexico, 5, 7

mule deer, 9, 13

North American Indians, 33, 35

predator, 9, 11, 15, 17, 18, 21, 23, 31, 33, 37, 40

rut, 25, 35

scent, 18, 29
scrape, 25, 27
smell, 18
speed, 11, 18
storm, 18

tail, 11, 21

velvet, 25

weight, 4, 10-11, 27
Winnebago Indians, 35-36
wolves, 18

United States, 4-5, 7, 9-10

yearling, 9, 29